HOW TO DIVIDE YOUR FAMILY'S ESTATE AND HEIRLOOMS PEACEFULLY AND SENSIBLY

A No-Nonsense, Solutions-Based Guide for Equitable Distribution

By Julie Hall
The Estate Lady®

The Estate Lady Publications
6420-A1 Rea Road #135, Charlotte NC 28277
www.theestatelady.com
704.543.1051

Credits:
Domna V. Colepaugh, Assistant

Library of Congress Control Number: 2010940077

ISBN: 978-0-9844191-2-8

Printed in the United States of America.

For rights or permissions inquiries, please contact
The Estate Lady® at Julie@TheEstateLady.com

For information about custom editions, special sales, premium or corporate packages, please contact The Estate Lady at 704.543.1051 or at Julie@TheEstateLady.com

For all my clients–
past, present and future.

Thank you for sharing your lives so I could
learn how to serve you in a greater capacity.

Table of Contents

About the Author

Julie Hall, author of *The Boomer Burden, Dealing With Your Parent's Lifetime Accumulation of Stuff*, and *A Boomer's Guide To Cleaning Out Your Parents' Estate in 30 Days or Less*, is an estate expert that specializes in personal property. As owner and operator of The Estate Lady®, LLC, which offers turnkey estate dissolution services, she brings eighteen years of experience to families facing the overwhelming task of sorting through and emptying their parents' home. Her expertise is called upon for consulting, conducting on-site estate sales, appraising personal property, and organizing the removal and disposal of contents in the most appropriate way.

In addition to her responsibilities as The Estate Lady®, Julie's passion for helping as many distressed families as possible deal with the challenges of estate dissolution inspired her to take ownership of the American Society of Estate Liquidators® (ASEL) in 2007. As director of ASEL, her vision is to dedicate the organization to being an educational and referral resource to estate liquidation professionals nationwide. Today, ASEL offers educational courses, resources, products, and support to industry professionals and those interested in becoming estate liquidators.

A popular speaker to groups dealing with older adult issues and estate accumulation challenges, she is also an expert author on many senior and boomer websites, answering questions about appraisals, downsizing, and family matters. Her work has been published in The Wall Street Journal, Bloomberg News, MSN Money, LA Times, etc, and she is called upon by people worldwide for her sound advice.

In 2007, The Estate Lady®, LLC was selected by StartupNation as one of the top three home-based businesses in the United States in its Boomers Back in Business category.

Julie is a member of the Certified Appraisers Guild of America, the National Speakers Association, the National Association of Women Business Owners, and the Better Business Bureau. Julie resides in Charlotte, North Carolina, with her family.

For more information, please visit Julie's websites: www.TheEstateLady.com, www.ASELonline.com, www.TheBoomerBurden.com, or her blog at http://estatelady.wordpress.com.

Introduction

With all my years in the estate industry, the one thing I kept hearing over and over is how my boomer clients wish they had a simple, step-by-step, "how to" guide to point them in the right direction after beloved parents become infirm and/or pass away. I have dedicated my career to being a resource for clients and empowering them with knowledge to take on the overwhelming responsibility of dividing a loved one's personal assets, but to do so with little or no fighting, and making sense of the madness.

I want you to be prepared for what's coming. There is much to do both before and after parents leave us. When the entire family understands the roles of heir and executor, and grasps the idea that this doesn't have to be a vicious process, dividing the estate will become more orderly and fair. I hope this guide will act as a friendly hand to hold during the process.

This guide is complimentary to my other books, *The Boomer Burden – Dealing With Your Parents' Lifetime Accumulation of Stuff,* and *A Boomer's Guide To Cleaning Out Your Parents' Estate in 30 Days or Less,* available on Amazon and major booksellers. *The Boomer Burden* hit #1 in several different categories, and its reviews are tremendous. People email me from all over the world thanking me for writing it. With 100+ million of us needing this guidance, I would recommend picking up these books if you have not yet done so. If you have already read it, this guide is an additional resource and will act as a working manual to put in your purse or briefcase to check things off as you go.

My goal is to make this daunting process as simple as possible for you, while giving you the tools you need to divide the estate equitably. You need a quick-reference, easy to understand, easy to follow guide that provides you with peace of mind and keeps it "simple."

I know this guide will offer you trustworthy guidance and lighten *your* load during this very challenging time in your life.

Section I

Getting Started: Principles for Dividing Your Parents' Estate

KNOWLEDGE IS POWER AND PEACE OF MIND

Being prepared and fully understanding what you are about to get into is a significant step towards assuring the process of dividing your parents' estate is one that brings your family closer together versus tearing it apart. The fact that you have purchased this guide, or that it was given to you, will give you the knowledge you need, so you can do the best possible job under these extenuating circumstances.

Following are some fundamental principles which are crucial to understand before you begin. These will ensure that the process is manageable and fair for everyone.

☐ **The Decedent has the First Right to Speak.**

Is there a valid will or trust? Are there specific bequests included with those documents? What's written in the will and other final documents guides this entire process. Often heirs squabble because nothing was written or documented; it becomes a matter of "Mom said I could have that" or "Dad always wanted me to have this." If mom or dad said that and no one else had knowledge they said it, it becomes a tug of war which ultimately leads to a tug of hearts.

Unfortunately, a verbal bequest is hearsay and does not have the validity of a written document; sometimes even a written document's validity is questioned. Many of my clients intentionally gift heirlooms and other possessions while they are still alive, which will relieve much of the pressure to divide after the loved one passes away.

If no will or trust was created or found, this process will certainly be more challenging but attainable, especially if the heirs are willing to work together through the process. Always consider the assistance of an estate planning attorney who specializes in this area of the law. If your loved one was working with an attorney or other professionals, it would be wise to contact them to see if they knew anything about the document's location, or if they even had a will.

☐ **Get the Facts & Documentation.**

☐ **Protect All Assets.**

It is not only important to have any critical documents in hand, but also to know **where all assets are** (including usernames, passwords, codes and keys) and **what they are**. This guide will help you know where to potentially find assets that may be hidden in unexpected places.

Important Principles to Guide You:

☐ **Never sell, give away, donate, or discard anything until a professional has looked at it first.** We see things of exorbitant value being thrown out and given away to friends and neighbors. Heirs either assume the items have no value, or they become hasty in trying to empty the house rapidly.

☐ **Equitable Distribution.** Among equals (siblings/heirs), what you do for one, you should do for all. Have all siblings send to the executor a wish list of what they would like to have. Once an appraiser has evaluated and written a report, the executor can put together a spreadsheet (sample wish list in the back of this book) and compare lists to make sure they are equitable in distribution. This ensures that no one person gets the lion's share.

☐ **Be Honest.** Be honest about any correspondence or conversations you have had with your parents regarding the disposition of certain items. Be honest about any items in your parents' home that may already belong to you or one of your siblings. Be honest about what is being taken from the home after the funeral. Be honest if you find mom's long lost diamond ring everyone has wondered about for years.

☐ **Be Fair.** It is not recommended that the heirs start helping themselves immediately. On the contrary, it is the responsibility of the executor to prevent that from happening until after the personal property is looked at and evaluated by a professional to ensure equitable distribution. Often the fighting begins when heirs take matters into their own hands. This is preventable when important rules are set in place and everybody plays fair.

☐ **Don't Take It Personally.** As difficult as this may be due to the emotional highs and lows which are normal and expected, make a promise not to take whatever transpires during the process personally. This will be crucial for your ability to move through the process effectively.

It is virtually guaranteed that at least one sibling or family member will show their true colors and make life pretty unbearable. They may even say things that are exceptionally hurtful and seem unforgivable. Try your best to remember that this treatment really has little to do with you and mostly stems from what is going on inside of them – unresolved issues, grief, pain from the past, etc. You just happen to be the target of these very powerful emotions. The next point is the reason why this is so important.

☐ **Understand the Pain Being Felt.** Pain is part of the process when grieving and coping with the loss of your parent(s) or another loved one. It will be a time of personal growth — making peace with anything left unsaid or unfinished, and cherishing old memories. Validate and listen to what siblings are feeling, and be honest with how you are feeling too.

☐ **Work Cooperatively.** Create an environment where you simply agree with your siblings upfront that you will do what mom and dad wanted. You will find it necessary to bite your tongue and turn the other cheek more than you would like to, but it is necessary. It is also important to share your thoughts and commit to work together as a team.

Imagine if you and your siblings/heirs were a team of horses all hitched up together with a common destination: concluding the estate settlement process amicably. Now, imagine you all started running in different directions because you all have different ideas. The result would be disastrous and there would certainly be injuries involved.

But if all of you can find a way to run in the same direction, on the same page and at the same time, you will find that the arrival to your destination will be much easier to attain.

☐ **Do the "Speed Limit."** Don't drag your feet unnecessarily in this process. On the other hand, you may have to wait with parts of this process, due to probate, identifying and settling debts, etc. Please check with an estate planning attorney, when in doubt.

□ **Approach the Division of Property with Reason and Restraint.** When dividing your parents' property, whether you are the executor or not, you must realize that some people will always be unreasonable and a challenge to you personally, as well as to the process. No matter how much logic you employ, you will still see behavior that will amaze you. Do your best to arm yourself with logical rationale and techniques.

□ **Document Everything.** This includes who gets what, both prior to and after a loved one's death. Document every gift and heirloom during the division of personal property.

□ **Do your best to work through the division of property in a timely manner.** Some children will hastily jump into the estate within hours of mom's passing. Others will take years to sort through every old coupon or matchbook. Somewhere between these two extremes is a balance that is appropriate. Be aware that financial needs may drive a family to divide property quicker than they desire; work together to meet those needs.

□ **Do recognize that you are all in the same boat.** Going in different directions is not an option. Cooperation is needed 100% of the time.

Do make careful decisions about storage. Placing estate items in storage is not always a good idea. While storage can be a good temporary solution, eventually a decision needs to be made as to the disposition of these items. We have a tendency to forget about what's in storage; you know the saying, "Out of sight, out of mind."

While these items are sitting in storage, either forgotten or due to delayed decisions, the monthly bills keep rolling in. That can add up to a substantial amount of expense. At some point, most people realize that the items they are keeping in storage are of less value than what it is costing them to rent the space.

Often people will keep items, which they feel have value or will increase in value, in storage for long periods of time. Generally, furniture doesn't do well in an environment that is not the same as your home. Items can be stacked or stored incorrectly. By the time we retrieve some of the items in storage, they have lost some value due to damage (heat, cold, humidity, mildew, mold, veneer coming off, plus numerous other issues).

Section II

To Heir is Human;
To Know Your Role is Priceless

YOU'RE ENTITLED TO NOTHING ... UNLESS IT IS GIVEN TO YOU

As an heir, you do have responsibilities and you need to give the executor the space he/she needs to do their job well. You also need to understand your rights, which I have found time and time again to be assumed and not fully understood. Here are some guidelines to help you understand what is expected of you and others as heirs.

Your Rights and Responsibilities as an Heir

Your Rights

Heirs have a tendency to take matters into their own hands when a loved one has just died or when an estate is being divided. This is a no-no. Hopefully if there is a will, it will help you understand what will take place so you can operate from a basis of knowledge and facts.

The executor will also guide you through the process of what will take place and when. You are not at an "all you can take" buffet. Go through the process correctly, with the guidance of an attorney or executor who will set the stage. Here's your checklist:

- ☐ You are entitled to nothing unless it is given to you or has been specifically gifted to you in person or in writing.

- ☐ You are not entitled to a commission or other fee for your work on the estate unless you are the Executor of the estate, or you have an agreement with the Executor to provide services for compensation.

- ☐ You are not entitled to see the last will and testament even if you are an immediate family member (i.e. spouse, children, siblings) or are mentioned in the will. Once a will is filed with the court, it is a matter of public record and may be examined by any interested person, whether a beneficiary or not. Forcing any person to show you the will before court filing will likely require the services of any attorney.

Your Responsibilities

☐ You should work with the executor to help assure that the process of collecting assets, satisfying debt claims, and distributing the remainder of the estate to beneficiaries goes as smoothly as possible.

☐ You should realize that the probate process has to run its due course. Whether the estate is large or small, the beneficiary should not expect to receive a final distribution of assets for 6 to 12 months, or longer.

☐ It's not about you! It's all about honoring your parents' wishes and going through this process in a respectful manner.

You may be reading this book because you have been charged with coordinating with the Executor or you may even be the Executor managing the division process. You may also be reading this to understand how to help or be of assistance as one of the rightful heirs or as a family friend. The role you play when dividing the estate's personal property can be of great value if handled in a manner that adheres to the principles discussed in Section I.

If There is No Will

Many older people assume that their children will work things out between themselves, and even if there are disagreements along the way, everything will eventually be fine. Unfortunately, when a person dies without a will (intestate), the state has the legal responsibility to handle the affairs of the deceased. The estate is immediately placed in probate court.

When there is no valid will, the probate court appoints an administrator to handle the decedent's affairs, and his or her property is distributed according to a formula fixed by that state's laws. There is no wiggle room in these laws, regardless of what proof you may have that Mom or Dad intended to leave the house to you. You will also have no control over the timeline; the court will.

After the taxes, funeral expenses, and administrative costs are paid, the remaining property is divided among the surviving family members, but not necessarily as the parent wanted. The laws in each state are very specific as to how the property is distributed when there is no will, including which relatives have priority.

For details of your particular state's intestate estate distribution laws, see the following website. http://www.mystatewill.com/

Every Heir Should DO the Following:

Here are some do's to consider as you step into the role of being an heir in order to keep peace, build collaboration, and expedite the division of the estate.

- ☐ **Do** honor your loved one. This is all about honoring your loved one who has died. Therefore, I recommend that a large photo of the loved one who has passed away is prominently displayed, so they are remembered and honored.

- ☐ **Do** have an open forum and gathering of all heirs together in one room to say what is on each person's mind, to set expectations based on the wishes of the deceased loved one, and also to confirm what everyone's role is within the family (what to expect from your siblings and other heirs). Having that talk at the beginning will alleviate many assumptions later on.

- ☐ **Do** recognize and acknowledge the emotions that go with the loss of the loved one and the attachment to the "stuff" left behind (sentimental vs. monetary, and everything in between).

- ☐ **Do** give siblings a chance to speak once about their family hurts and emotional challenges. After issues have been raised and aired, let go of the hurt and challenge and move forward. There's no need to keep repeating them.

- ☐ **Do** encourage everyone to be a part of the healing in the way that is best for them. This is not about taking sides. This is about being objective and helping family members work through their hurt, if a particular possession is not being given to them, or whatever the hurt might be during the process.

- ☐ **Do** understand and confirm the values of the different types of personal property before being divided among the heirs. It is imperative that you bring in an objective third party - a personal property appraiser - to assign values to the estate contents.

☐ **Do** realize that prices you find on the internet are not always accurate. Those are asking prices, and anyone can ask any price they wish. If you are going online to research what an item is worth, you must find what the item is actually *selling for*.

☐ **Do** leave the gossip and innuendos at the door. Don't waste energy and time talking about this one's bad behavior or that someone is more deserving or undeserving. This only fuels animosity, future discontent, and other relational problems.

☐ **Do** bring a positive attitude into the process. This can make or break the situation. Be committed that everyone will be positive, supportive, and considerate to one another.

☐ **Do** be solutions-based in how you approach every challenge. For each problem, there is a solution. Do your best to get into and stay in a solutions-based mindset.

☐ **Do** make a pact that no greed is allowed. Show greed to the door.

☐ **Do** consult a professional counselor, minister, rabbi, or other advisor (if needed) when in doubt, and feeling uncertain about how to handle a particular situation that arises.

☐ **Do** create wish lists of items you would like to have, with the understanding that there are no guarantees what you will ultimately receive, unless it was bequeathed to you.

☐ **Do** be prepared that tensions will be high and the environment will be uncomfortable due to the mixture of personalities and hidden agendas. True colors and fangs will be revealed during this process, so don't be surprised when this occurs.

Dividing possessions can be among the most contentious experiences in our adult lives. There is no way to completely eliminate family squabbles, but you can learn to minimize them. Don't sweat the small stuff. Keep emotions from smoldering into flames that will never be totally extinguished, once unkind things are said and hurtful actions are done.

Every Heir Should NOT DO the Following:

Here are some don'ts to consider as you step into the role of being an heir in order to keep peace, build collaboration, and expedite the division of the estate.

- ☐ **Don't** take anything or give anything away until you call in a professional and all has been valuated.

- ☐ **Don't** include in-laws in the division process. Immediate siblings come first and in-laws should respectively stay out of it.

- ☐ **Don't** take things just to take them.

- ☐ **Don't** take items in anticipation of what your children will want.

- ☐ **Don't** be a victim and be suckered into giving things to acquaintances. Give what you and your siblings agree on.

- ☐ **Don't** help yourself to anything in the estate without the executor's approval.

- ☐ **Don't** use your key to go in the house and take what you feel entitled to.

- ☐ **Don't** start taking things while your parents are still alive without your siblings' or other family members' knowledge. Even if mom or dad gives it to you, always be forthright and inform the others.

- ☐ **Don't** do or say anything that might hurt another heir intentionally.

- ☐ **Don't** be part of the problem.

- ☐ **Don't** be impatient. This is a very tedious process fraught with emotional expectations. Everyone needs to do their best to work together.

- ☐ **Don't** expect to get everything you would like to have.

☐ **Don't** believe that just because it's old, it's valuable. Get the facts from a professional.

☐ **Don't** badger the executor. Certainly it may appear as if the executor is procrastinating and in some cases, they might be. Understand that this process is time consuming. The executor must wait for certain timetables and events to take place. Sometimes they have to wait for answers from other professionals and are at the mercy of someone else's schedule. Also, each individual state has its own timetable of what has to take place and when.

☐ **Don't** be a martyr. If you want something, ask politely. No regrets or bringing it up later.

☐ **Don't** rush your decisions on what you would like to have from the estate.

☐ **Don't** break up sets if you can help it, for example, china, crystal, silver flatware, etc.

☐ **Don't** confuse sentimental value with monetary value.

Ethics and Etiquette

Following these simple rules of etiquette and ethics will help you and your family to keep the peace, love, compassion, and trust flowing throughout the process:

- The Executor should set the expectations and share the overall process with the heirs present during an initial meeting. If they cannot all be physically present due to distance, arrange a conference call. At the very least, all heirs should be emailed or sent letters detailing the process, and all documents should go out at the same time to each heir.

- Agree that everyone will do everything they can to keep the peace while being fair and honest.

- Always seek to take the "high road" in any given situation, which will make it a win-win for everyone.

- Agree that all potential treasures or unique finds discovered during the cleaning and dividing process will be fully disclosed to all heirs for determination of distribution and proper valuation appraisal.

- Understand any laws that dictate how personal property is to be handled within your state, especially if there is no will or no specific bequests associated with the will. Sometimes probate can take quite a while and in some cases, personal property division can be held up until that is sorted out.

- Be willing to forfeit an item you really wanted in order to keep the peace. (But keep it equitable -- no one should get the lion's share)

- It is best when this only involve siblings -- no in-laws, no grandchildren -- no matter how well-meaning they are. Keep it simple. The more people that are involved, the more complex become the issues.

Section III

The Role of the Executor: Don't Execute the Executor

THE ROLE OF THE EXECUTOR

☐ The executor has the responsibility to protect all that the decedent owned until all decisions have been made about the proper distribution and dissolution methods.

☐ The executor must also gather all the estate assets, which includes retrieving money or other types of property that were loaned to others.

☐ The executor must locate the will and begin to see that its wishes are fulfilled. It is his/her responsibility to identify the values of those assets, secure those assets, and distribute them in accordance with the will.

☐ The executor is in control of all of the decedent's assets and is *the only one authorized* to collect and transfer the assets. This task is stressful, quite complicated, and exceptionally time consuming.

☐ The executor must make sure that everything required from a legal perspective has been done, according to estate laws in the state where the estate is located.

☐ The executor's job is a thankless one. Keep this in mind if you are one of the heirs. If you are also playing the dual role of an heir and an executor, my heart goes out to you, as you will be watched very closely. Go forward with objectivity and fairness. Do everything you can to carry out the wishes of the decedent in an honorable way.

☐ Compensation of the executor

When the executor is part of the family or a beneficiary, he/she can forego the statutory executor's fee, if they choose. Fees are state specific, and normally set as a percentage of the estate (1% to 4% in smaller estates). These fees are regulated by probate court and state law, and come out of the estate. When the executor is a non-beneficiary (bank or lawyer), expect that they will charge the maximum fee allowed by state law, even in an uncomplicated estate.

THE RESPONSIBILITES OF THE EXECUTOR

The following actions are important and critical steps to be taken by the executor (or estate attorney), in order to properly protect and prepare the estate on behalf of the decedent.

PROTECT THE ESTATE

☐ Collect keys / change residential and other property locks. Always change the locks because you never know who has keys.

☐ New master keys should be in the executor's and/or estate attorney's possession only.

☐ Notify heirs and family members that locks have been changed for security reasons.

☐ Oversee collection of all necessary paperwork. <u>Note</u>: A detailed listing of the paperwork to be collected can be found in *A Boomer's Guide to Cleaning Out Your Parents' Estate in 30 Days or Less* by Julie Hall.

☐ Remove valuables from the estate for temporary safekeeping. This should only be done by the executor or executrix.

☐ Notify heirs and family that removal of valuables is temporary, and only until the division process begins.

☐ Prepare a list of all valuables to be kept in executor's or estate attorney's file as documentation.

PREPARE THE ESTATE

☐ All communication with heirs needs to be documented throughout this process.

☐ Hire a professional appraiser to assess all valuables.

□ Walk through the house and list anything of sentimental value.

□ Walk through the house and locate anything listed as a bequest in the will.

□ Make a copy of the created list to distribute to heirs for review.

□ Have heirs prepare a wish list of items deemed not to be sold that they would like to have.

□ Divide contents fairly among heirs, using appraised values, to assure equitable distribution.

□ Manage and oversee assignment of any item that has not been bequeathed, when several heirs want the same item.

□ Notify heirs and family of how and when estate will be managed and dispersed once determined.

□ Gather all professionals pertinent to the estate's dissolution.

□ Set strict deadlines for wish lists, papers to be signed, and any other documentation necessary for the process to continue to move forward.

□ Set a date to empty the house. <u>Note</u>: An extensive discussion of this process can be found in *A Boomer's Guide to Cleaning Out Your Parents' Estate in 30 Days or Less* by Julie Hall.

□ Understand that not everyone is going to agree, comply, or go with the flow of this process.

□ Document everything to cover yourself, and keep documents well organized in files.

LEGAL HIGHLIGHTS FOR EXECUTORS

☐ A 6 to 12 month period would be an average goal for making all distributions from an estate and closing it.

☐ Partial distributions are common, and tangible personal property is usually distributed pretty quickly.

☐ However, the Executor still has a fiduciary duty to assure that all of the debts are taken care of before distributing property, even tangible personal property, to the beneficiaries.

☐ In many states, a procedure is used to notify all creditors of the death, giving them a period of 3 months to submit any claims for payment of debts. The procedure involves notice by publication for unknown creditors, and actual notice to creditors of which the Executor has specific knowledge.

☐ In many states, an executor who distributes property before this 3-month period is at risk if the assets are not sufficient to satisfy all of the debts. The executor can have personal liability for the debts in this situation.

☐ The executor would not want to distribute any valuable items until he/she is sure that all debts (including taxes) can be paid with the funds that will remain. The liability, in most cases, would be limited to the value of the items. If you are distributing items of modest value, the risk would be correspondingly low.

Section IV

What's it Worth?
Values and Expectations

SENTIMENTAL VALUE

Sometimes a piece doesn't have much monetary value, but it does have priceless sentimental value to someone left behind. When Lisa was a little girl, her mother sat beside her on her bed each night and brushed her long hair. This was their special time together and they talked about everything which moms and daughters talk about: what happened at school that day, the boy she had a crush on, and all the hows and whys of life.

Her mom would tuck her in, pull the covers up around her neck, and then say a little prayer they had memorized. Sometimes her mom would sing a little song that Lisa always remembered. It made sense that of all the things her mother left, Lisa went straight for the brush that her mother kept for all those years. That brush didn't have any monetary value, but triggered those wonderful memories between her and her mom from all those years ago. So to Lisa, it might as well have come from Fort Knox because to her, it was priceless.

As you go through your parents' home to divide the belongings among the family members, you should first look for those items that carry special meaning. But a serious word of caution: Exercise some careful judgment and restraint because if you're not careful, you will haul away a trailer full of stuff. Ultimately, this stuff will just be stashed away someplace; it may even cause marital strife when you bring home more belongings.

For Lisa, that one brush will sit on her own dresser and remind her each day of her mother. Usually, two or three items that have sentimental value are all you need. Look for those things that have special meaning and that can either be displayed where you will see them or can actually be used.

In the long run, you can't take it with you either, and then the stuff falls to your children. The younger generations have little care or tolerance towards all this stuff. It is better that you make wise choices now.

Sentimental value may even be the highest measure of value for some people. Still, when most people face the daunting task of dividing the property of their parents' home, they see dollar signs.

MONETARY VALUE

There certainly can be items of significant value in your parents' estate. They may have old appraisals done years ago; yet they may not even know they have something of value tucked away in a closet. I recommend that you get new appraisals to reflect current market values. Market values will differ from state to state, as will the level of desirability in the market and the overall economic situation.

Hire a personal property appraiser to write a formal report on the items he/she feels have significant value in the home. Often, the children have heard stories passed down through the generations that, for example, great grandfather's handmade bench is exceptionally valuable because it is old. It is important to note: ***just because an item is old doesn't necessarily mean it's valuable***. There are many contributing factors to value, and a professional appraiser will know all of them.

By the same token, it is not unusual for families to feel mom and dad just kept a bunch of junk, only to discover a $60,000 vase in the basement among the myriad piles of National Geographic magazines. This is a wonderful example of *monetary* value and why you need an appraiser!

On the flip side, heirs are often very surprised to learn the monetary values of their parents' estates may not be as much as they originally thought or hoped. The average on-site estate sale brings in between $6,000 and $20,000, with the majority being around $8,000 to $12,000. Most people are disappointed at the limited monetary value of the things their parents left behind. Let's look at some of the factors that influence or affect monetary value.

FACTORS THAT AFFECT MONETARY VALUE

- **What is something really worth?** Ultimately, whatever someone is willing to give you for it.

- **Is it just junk, or something more?** The TV cable shows will have you believe there is treasure in everyone's estate. While you may find interesting collectibles, not every estate contains a significant monetary treasure. However, sometimes the most unsuspecting and modest home will have one or two pieces that are really spectacular and no one knew it.

- **Never judge a book by its cover.** It might be pretty to look at but it might not have much value. Again, sometimes the most unsuspecting (and often unattractive) items may have more value than you know. All that glitters is not gold.

Antique, Vintage, Collectible?

When discussing the monetary value of items, consider whether they are antique, vintage, or collectible. Though these terms have complex meanings and effect on value, here is a brief overview:

- Antique refers to an item that is at least one hundred years old.

- Vintage describes older items that are not yet one hundred years old. Generally, vintage items are seen in antique stores and considered collectible. Vintage pieces are original to the period that produced them and are not reproductions.

- Collectible refers to anything people collect, usually older items on their way to become antique.

These terms are often misunderstood and improperly used. When determining the value of any item, it is always best to consult a professional appraiser.

The Law of Supply and Demand

This law pretty much sets the standard for everything, everywhere, and at all times. If we have too much of something on the market, china sets for example, the price is driven downward as it is currently. There are too many sets in the marketplace and not enough demand. The younger generations don't want grandma's china; they want their own sets from IKEA; they can afford to change color and pattern every two years as they want.

If something is in demand (remember all those collector plates?), the prices are driven upwards because people want to collect them. So the manufacturer cranks them out by the millions. People buy these plates because they think they will go up in value, but too many are made. Eventually, the result is that the supply far exceeds the demand, and the prices fall dramatically.

Such is the case with many things we find in estates. What mom paid in 1980 has no bearing on what it's worth now. It might have gone up if it is exceptional and rare, but most likely, it has gone down. Keep an open mind and reasonable expectations based on the professional's valuation. This is vital, because not everything is going to be as you expect which will lead to disappointment.

A professional appraiser looks for things like:

Marketability ~ What's hot, and what's not, in the current market? Depression glass is no longer the "cat's meow", but vintage and antique toys seem to be holding their value. Appraisers watch and understand the market trends and they can advise what has value and what doesn't. This will be of great assistance when trying to decide what to keep and what to sell.

Collectability ~ Ultimately, it is the collectors who set the stage for prices. Somewhat related to marketability, if an item belongs to a category of objects that people desire and collect, it *could* increase in value, but not always. Collectability can also be short-lived. Remember the Beanie Babies? The demand fell after a while, but supply was still abundant, and prices took a nosedive.

When a famous celebrity dies, everyone goes out and buys millions of memorabilia items. They somehow believe that their items will increase in value. However, millions are produced to make millions of people believe that their items will increase in value. This is why we find thousands of collector plates in estates. People paid $29.99 or more for each one, believing they would increase in value. Today, you see the majority of them on the internet for less than $5.00 each.

Age ~ Remember, just because it is old doesn't mean it's valuable. Age is a contributing factor to value and can play an important role, depending on the item. Here's another compelling reason to hire an appraiser. Antiques have always held a special interest for many people, but the market is not nearly as strong as it was once. Most families are not aware of market trends; antiques must be valuated appropriately. Remember too, internet prices often do not reflect the realized prices, which are the prices the items *actually sold for*. Do not be fooled by what someone is asking for the item; this may not match the item's value.

Condition ~ It might be really old and different, but if the original purpose of the piece has been disturbed or altered (painted, re-glued, refinished, stripped, repaired, new pieces added, etc.) the condition will affect the value, sometimes more than you would think.

Collectors generally want as close to original condition as possible. They do not want a 100 year old bronze sculpture that has been polished to a perfect luster. They want an old bronze sculpture with patina: that wonderful mellow color that can only come from age and proves it's been around a very long time. Since it isn't a new item, it shouldn't look new and should be left in original condition.

Many items we find in estates from the Depression Era have antique metals that have all been polished and even lacquered permanently so they can't tarnish. This will have a fairly large impact on value.

Rarity ~ So many families feel they have something in the estate that is rare. Rare means "extraordinary", clearly beyond unique and unusual. Rare is like a flawless diamond, exceptionally hard to find. Most of what we see in estates are what we call unique, but not extraordinary. But again, it's all relative.

Someone has to want to buy the item. If the item you have is rare and several people want it, the price will go up. But even if you have something rare but no one wants it because the demand is not there, then the selling price will not be very high.

Provenance ~ In estates, this is the *proven history* of an item. It is what professionals look for as the record or history of past ownership of an item or collection. It can be a document, photographic proof, signatures, or other evidence. Professionals are trained to look for comparable sales which may include auction records and other documented sales which will compare similar items within a similar period of time. Provenance could mean the difference between having $100.00 antique rifle or a rifle owned by Wild Bill Hickok. It's all in the proof.

Material ~ The material used to make something is also important. Is it a rare gemstone or glass? Is it exotic wood or plain pine? The material the artisan chooses, and the craftsmanship the artisan put into that material, are very important. More expensive and desirable materials generally mean the artist's work was, and still is, more valuable and desired among collectors. Some of the materials that seem to hold their value are gold, platinum, diamonds, sterling silver, ivory, coral, fine jade, exceptional furniture with inlaid marquetry and craftsmanship.

Style ~ Styles of almost everything have come and gone through the ages. What was once the rage is now obsolete. This truth applies to furniture styles and hair styles; some are classic and some are fads. Some people prefer the simplicity of primitives, while others adore the complexity of Rococo.

Whichever style is popular at the time affects the value of the piece. For example, if you have good floral upholstered furniture from the 1980's or 1990's, the demand is very low and so are the prices. Remember as a result, you always have the viable option of donating these pieces to a charity and taking the tax deduction.

Handmade vs. Factory made ~ Several times a day, an heir will call and say they have a mahogany dining room suite from the 1940s that belonged to their parents. The pieces are sturdy and pretty, and the heirs are expecting more from these pieces than they should. The majority of our parents have them, and they were factory made in mass quantities. But they are out of favor with today's styles.

Hand made pieces certainly find favor with today's collectors, even with imperfections. Collectors say they can feel the passion that was put into the making of such a piece. Since it was not mass produced and may only be one of a handful made, this piece may indeed have value.

Collectible, Vintage, and Antique Items that May Have Value

Here is a brief list of the types of things you should look for in your parents' estate: antique, vintage or collectible items that have remained consistent in the market. This is only the tip of the iceberg. You should have them all evaluated by a personal property appraiser.

Advertising items (signs, posters, giveaways)
Art
Art pottery and glass
Art Deco items
Arts and Crafts Movement items
Art Nouveau items
Barbie dolls
Baseball cards/sports memorabilia
Black Americana
Books (first editions, leather, antique)
Cameras, photographic equipment
Christmas items (antique, vintage)
Clothing
Coin and stamp collections
Cookie jars
Crystal (antique/signed)
Dolls and accessories
European figurines
Fishing lures
Fountain pens
Furniture
Glassware
Gold/silver/precious metals
Guns
Inkwells
Jewelry (costume, signed pieces, and genuine jewelry)
Kitchenware (vintage)

Lace/crochet work
Ladies' compacts/perfumes/vanity items
Lamps
Linens (some)
Lionel trains (original)
Mantel clocks and long case clocks
Mid-century items
Movie posters
Oriental items
Paperweights, preferably signed near base or on bottom
Photos
Pocket watches (railroad or genuine gold)
Porcelain (Meissen, etc.)
Postcards (antique)
Primitives (folk art)
Quilts
Radios
Railroad memorabilia
Rugs
Sculptures (signed, original)
Tapestries, textiles, and samplers
Tobaccoiana (smoking collectibles)
Tools
Toys
War/military memorabilia

Taken from *The Boomer Burden* by Julie Hall ©2007 by Thomas Nelson, Nashville, TN

SETTING EXPECTATIONS

Now that you have a better understanding of what items may be worth, it is important to note that your siblings, or other heirs involved, may disagree. The meeting of the minds can often begin as an arduous journey. Preparing for attack, even if it doesn't happen, is a good strategy to employ, just in case you need it.

You and your sibling(s) may have always been close. But now something doesn't feel right. They have said or done something to really cause some problems. This is common and expected, but it always catches you off guard.

The following fable, by an unknown author, predicts some of the behavior you will see in estates, even when you feel you have a close family. Anytime you have a combination of death, money, grief and potential greed, you have a dangerous recipe that needs to be disarmed as quickly as possible.

The Fable of the Frog and Scorpion
Author unknown

One day, a scorpion looked around at the mountain where he lived and decided that he wanted a change. So he set out on a journey through the forests and hills. He climbed over rocks and under vines and kept going until he reached a river.

The river was wide and swift, and the scorpion stopped to reconsider the situation. He couldn't see any way across. So he ran upriver and then checked downriver, all the while thinking that he might have to turn back.

Suddenly, he saw a frog sitting in the rushes by the bank of the stream on the other side of the river. He decided to ask the frog for help getting across the stream.

"Hello-o-o Mr. Frog!" called the scorpion across the water, "Would you be so kind as to give me a ride on your back across the river?"

"Well now, Mr. Scorpion! How do I know that if I try to help you, you won't try to kill me?" asked the frog hesitantly.

"Because," the scorpion replied, "If I try to kill you, then I would die too, for you see, I cannot swim!"

Now this seemed to make sense to the frog. But he asked. "What about when I get close to the bank? You could still try to kill me and get back to the shore!"

"This is true," agreed the scorpion, "But then I wouldn't be able to get to the other side of the river!"

"Alright then...how do I know you won't just wait till we get to the other side and THEN kill me?" said the frog.

"Ah-h-h...," crooned the scorpion, "Because you see, once you've taken me to the other side of this river, I will be so grateful for your help, that it would hardly be fair to reward you with death, now would it?!"

So the frog agreed to take the scorpion across the river. He swam over to the bank and settled himself near the mud to pick up his passenger. The scorpion crawled onto the frog's back, his sharp claws pricking into the frog's soft hide, and the frog slid into the river. The muddy water swirled around them, but the frog stayed near the surface so the scorpion would not drown. He kicked strongly through the first half of the stream, his flippers paddling wildly against the current.

Halfway across the river, the frog suddenly felt a sharp sting in his back and, out of the corner of his eye, saw the scorpion remove his stinger from the frog's back. A deadening numbness began to creep into his limbs.

"You fool!" croaked the frog, "Now we shall both die! Why on earth did you do that?"

The scorpion shrugged. "I could not help myself. It is my nature."

Then they both sank into the muddy waters of the swiftly flowing river.

Moral of the story: In almost every estate, you may uncover scorpion-like behavior in a family member, friend, or neighbor. Watch your back and be prepared.

Not everything is as it appears. While you may feel you have a very close knit family where all of the siblings get along, I can almost guarantee you that disagreements, hard feelings, and resentment will pop up along the way. Just when you think you know someone really well, they will do or say something to shock you during this process.

Look for clues in the faces and behaviors of the other heirs. Is it normal or out of character for them? Is someone being very quiet when they are normally extroverted? Is the sweet little sister who never says much suddenly obnoxiously boisterous and exceptionally difficult? Carefully study faces, body language, and what is spoken or written.

Look for these clues and try to put the fire out before it gets too big. It's much easier to put out a small fire that just started than to wait until after it has wiped out the forest. By then, the damage is done, unfixable and unforgettable.

WHAT TO DO FIRST

☐ **Have this talk with yourself and with siblings, prior to the division process.** This should take place under the executor's control and abide by what the will stipulates. All the heirs should agree to simply do their best to keep the peace. Certain guidelines, which must be met by all, should be set forth by the executor. The executor may consider suggestions from the heirs if their intentions are thoughtful and kind.

One example: "It would be a good idea if we could all meet and understand the process of dividing mom's estate. We need to choose the method on how to proceed with the division process. We need to draw up basic guidelines that all of us must follow, and we need to agree to work together."

☐ If the executor hasn't already done so, **ask each *immediate* heir to fill out a wish list** and give them a due date for when you need them back. Explain this is not a guarantee they are going to get these items ~ only a listing in which to figure out who wants what, based on financial equity. You will find a blank wish list in Section XII at the back of this guide.

☐ Once the wish lists are complete, **put together a spreadsheet with the immediate heirs' names and what items they desire.** It is good to distribute this spreadsheet to the heirs. Just make sure the totals under each heir's name are as equitable as possible. You will find a sample completed wish list in Section XII at the back of this guide.

☐ **Hire an appraiser to assign a value to each item** on the wish lists so they can be divided equitably.

☐ **Determine an organized and methodical way for the selection process of estate pieces.** Some executors may decide to use the birth order to select pieces and then the baby of the family picks twice as the order is reversed. If all the heirs filled out wish lists and those items have been evaluated by an appraiser, the division process may be a little easier, unless two or more heirs want the same item (see page 64).

Ways to Divide Personal Property

The following list provides some practical ways to divide personal property between heirs. These are all methods which clients have used in the past; some are favored, some are reckless and create difficulties.

Here are the only methods that I recommend.

1. Create a wish list based on equitable distribution; values should be known first. If the executor asks for this wish list ahead of time and gets the items appraised, the distribution can proceed according to the lists, but with no guarantee. Total value for each heir must be equivalent. Items are distributed when everyone is together and everyone is cooperative.
2. Heirs can purchase items based on appraised values and the money collected is then split evenly.
3. Distribute according to the decedent's written wishes.
4. Gift prior to infirmity or death.

Here are other methods which have been used, but which I don't necessarily recommend.

5. Items are selected by heirs in the order of their birth, then reverse order, i.e. 1, 2, 3, 3, 2, 1, etc.
6. Some families flip a coin, pick numbers out of a hat, select the highest card, etc. Children and siblings go first, then grandchildren, then extended family and friends.
7. Family auction: know the values of items first. Everyone starts out with a set amount of play money. You then bid against one another for the item(s) you want. When you are out of money, you are done.
8. A total liquidation of all assets; the cash proceeds are then divided by the number of heirs.

☐ Try to make sure **all heirs collect their items on the same day** when everyone is present. This way, no one can come into the home ahead of time or be accused of taking something that is not rightfully theirs.

☐ **Take this opportunity to discuss potential disagreements between siblings.** Before the division begins, acknowledge potential problems that might arise.

☐ **Keep it simple and stick with immediate heirs only.** When in the midst of setting the expectations, clear boundaries need to be drawn that the division is <u>with and among heirs only</u>. The children of the decedent would be the direct heirs in the most common scenario.

Involving in-laws often causes great concern and more tension than most families realize. In-laws need to remain quietly in the background, away from these private meetings. The selection process should be between siblings only.

☐ **Grandchildren should wait their turn.** Grandchildren can get involved a little later in the process. While they are family, grandchildren can really cause difficulties and family strife during the division process. It is perfectly fine to take one of your turns to choose things for your children, the decedent's grandchildren, but not "double dip." (One for me and one for my child)

Keep grandchildren out of it until the immediate siblings have made their selections and everyone knows the guidelines. It is not okay for them to be present during the beginning phase of discussions, and not okay for them to get more than other grandchildren.

☐ **Make sure no one takes anything without the executor's knowledge** and approval and without informing the other heirs. It could set someone off if one sibling keeps helping themselves without the others' knowledge.

☐ **During the day of division, all heirs should be present** and accounted for if at all possible, even if they only come to arrange to have their items shipped back home.

Section V

Tools to Minimize Family Fighting

LET COOL HEADS PREVAIL.
BE THE PEACE BROKER WHEN
FIGHTING OCCURS.

Perception is everything! Often, fights stem from assumptions made from misinformation and misunderstandings that could have been avoided or minimized.

Not long ago, I had a client who was ill and knew her time was approaching. She was also quite wealthy and her five children already began to swarm closer to mother. But she knew her children well and knew what was at stake. Unbeknown to her children, she worked closely with an estate planning attorney who was also her executor. She said she chose this attorney because he would be an objective third party who would fulfill her wishes and could stand up to her children who would be pushy. Furthermore, she did not want to choose one child to be the executor, as she knew that the executor would have to contend with pressure from the other children.

My client was very wise. When it came time for the will to be read to the children, her wishes were very clear. She was the one who made the decisions about who got what between her businesses and personal property. But there was one line that got everybody behaving:

"If anyone causes any trouble whatsoever ~ complains, argues, accuses, insults, makes faces, etc., they are to be given a $1.00 bill and escorted out, as that is all they will receive."

Don't you know all of those children sat like soldiers and never once acted up? They behaved, at least in front of the attorney. Mom had spoken and they listened, because so much was at stake.

Here are some ways to keep the peace and minimize disagreements:

☐ Call a family meeting where all heirs can gather together with the executor, either in person on via telephone, to set the parameters for the estate division process before it gets underway.

☐ If there are any underlying family disputes that have been going on for years, attempt to confirm that these disputes will not enter into the division process and need to be let go. This is very important to the success of this process!

☐ Document all communications throughout the process. Any conversations related to personal property should be documented and shared with all who may be affected. Document all phone calls.

☐ Once bequests are identified, have each heir apparent create a wish list. Prepare a spreadsheet that shares all wishes for an overall comparison and review. NOTE: The wish list worksheet has been provided in the back of this guide.

☐ Agree in advance, when multiple heirs desire the same item, how this will be handled. Will you share, obtain the value and sell the item, determine agreeable exchanges, or draw a name out of a hat? If several options could apply, prioritize them based on a mutually-agreed-upon protocol.

☐ Hire a professional personal property appraiser to valuate the items rather than having family members attempt to guess values. This will give this process due diligence.

The ideal way to avoid many disputes is to include your parents in the discussion of the estate and distribution of possessions, prior to their infirmity, mental decline, or death. If you are reading this in preparation for the inevitable, I commend you and encourage you to make this meeting with your parents a priority, to help make the estate settlement process easier down the road.

WHAT TO DO IF FIGHTING BREAKS OUT

With emotions and expectations high, there will be disputes and unexpected flair-ups. Here are some quick ways to handle situations as they arise:

- ☐ Clearly identify the source of the dispute or the bearer of the problem.

- ☐ Remain calm and attempt to hear both sides of the story and understand the situation.

- ☐ Validate the feelings of the individuals involved, but ask both to consider possible solutions. Then, select the most appropriate solution.

- ☐ Become a master of delegation by rallying others to help in possible resolutions.

- ☐ Once resolved, let it be done; reach an agreement by all that it is now in the past and do not allow it to be brought up repeatedly.

- ☐ Gently remind everyone involved that this is about the loved one's wishes, not our own.

UNFORTUNATE FAST FACTS

Share these statistics among family members to help them see the sad reality. A commitment by all to honor each other and the memory of your parents will take this journey through property division into a positive outcome:

- The most likely person to exploit the elderly is a family member or someone familiar to them.
- 60 percent of those financially abusing the elderly are adult children (National Elder Abuse Incidence Study).
- The cost of contesting a will often depletes the value of the property being contested.
- Five million cases of financial abuse of the elderly are reported each year (NPR).
- 1.1 percent of Americans receive $50,000 to $100,000 in inheritance; 1.1 percent receive more than $100,000; 91.9 percent receive nothing.

THE MANY FACES THAT EMERGE WHEN THE DIVIDING BEGINS

The Grief-Stricken Heir

It goes without saying that most heirs are genuinely grieving. It should also go without saying that because they are grieving, they are not quite themselves - in body, mind or spirit - and the feeling of being out of balance may last weeks, months or even the remainder of their lives. People are not themselves when mourning the recent loss of a loved one, especially if they had a particularly close relationship with the departed and will feel completely out of sorts, especially when the loss is recent. But not every child or heir will really grieve. Some just want the goods.

As a professional in the estate world who has witnessed all forms of grief and how it will often show itself to family members, I find there are two basic types of grief:
1) The genuine type where family members are hurting and really should be supporting one another through the loss, or
2) The type that enables an heir to get more from the estate if they put on a really good show of being grief stricken.

The latter will often be discovered early by other heirs who are sincerely in a place of mourning. The accusations begin to fly and everyone's ideas and feelings come to a head, causing the "mother of all confrontations."

The reason I bring this to your attention is for you to be aware of emotions coming to a head sooner rather than later. Just expect the unexpected.

The Guilt-Ridden Heir

Guilt, and the shame that often accompanies it, is one of the heaviest burdens to carry through life. Much of it will come to a head when the last remaining parent dies. Issues we thought would never rise again suddenly pop up as problems within ourselves, with our siblings, or with other relatives.

It continues to amaze me just how many people are prepared to willingly carry guilt throughout their lives as if it were attached to them. Those who choose not to deal with it appropriately, or seek professional guidance to lighten their load, will live their life with a heavy boulder on their back. It is wise to seek professional counsel so you can live a normal life.

In order to overcome guilt, it is important to first understand and uncover the root causes, and many people just don't want to *go there*. I have seen guilt come from certain behaviors within a family and it may also come from fears (some irrational) and from personal belief systems.

Guilt can cause you or a loved one to have blocked memories from childhood. It is not surprising then, that these issues come to a head when clearing out the family home, and need to be dealt with.

Bewildering behaviors will suddenly appear; it is important to recognize that what you are witnessing is a memory a sibling is dealing with, which may have been suppressed for decades. These behaviors can be particularly unruly and very challenging when going through the family home, as a flood of memories revive themselves as you go through mom and dad's possessions.

Just be aware that a sibling or heir may be experiencing guilt, especially if they didn't have much to do with the loved one, are geographically remote and couldn't help much, or they may have been estranged at one time, or are still estranged when their parent dies.

The guilty relative may have had a good relationship with the loved one, but for whatever reason did not have as much interaction as he now wishes had been the case. This person also may have been absent during the difficult weeks or months leading up to the parent's death, because he didn't know how to handle the situation.

This relative will try to be cooperative, but will often mask resentment for having to help tie up loose ends. He will either act out his anger toward other family members or blame himself for not being there when he was needed. Either way, he could create problems for other family members.

The "Do-Gooder" Heir

They are exceptionally well organized and can move mountains in a short period of time. The Do-Gooder generally means well and will often pick up the slack when another relative is less than prepared for the task at hand.

A Do-Gooder may, or may not, have inappropriate motives. Most Do-Gooders are very helpful and responsible, but sometimes they can take things too personally, and be too responsible (and do too much without the other siblings present).

This can anger other siblings, or at the very least, irritate them. Any form of irritation or annoyance can fuel a full-blown argument at anytime during this process.

There are also Do-Gooders whose motives are improper. They get into the estate prior to anyone else to get dibs on the good stuff. They will often remove items before any of the other siblings have a chance to sort through the possessions. This is not recommended; it is up to the executor to keep everyone in check.

The Hoarder Heir

The cable networks would have us believing that any hoarder will let us into their homes willingly because they desperately want their homes cleared out, right? Wrong! The majority of hoarders will not allow anyone in, including family, let along a camera crew. To make matters worse, no one is allowed in until the Hoarder actually dies.

Some families feel forced to call in law enforcement to have the loved one removed from the dangerous environment. Others slowly become estranged not really knowing how to deal with it, so they don't do anything. It is the most overwhelming situation any family can face when having to empty the family home.

We have seen hoarder's homes that are so dangerous they need to be torn down. The city will come in and condemn the home to be destroyed. The family will then have a set period of time to recover or salvage any items from the home.

If the home is not a tear-down, the family faces exceptionally high bills to have the home cleaned out by professionals. Yet, these professionals will know the who, what, where and when of how to proceed. It is important to note that many homes of hoarders can be a bio-hazard, and the proper breathing apparatus/masks, boots, gloves or Tyvek® suits may be required to do the job.

The Unscrupulous Heir (Thief)

Hard as it may be to believe this, there is usually one found in most families. Heirs will go into the estate at night and go through items before the others. Heirs have even cleared out the home overnight unbeknown to their siblings, or they have changed locks without informing anyone.

> ➤ Only the executor is responsible for changing locks. The executor should notify everyone that this was done to protect the assets. Sometimes numerous neighbors, caregivers, etc., will have keys, and this is a excellent way to prevent anything from disappearing.

There are other ways to be unscrupulous: A sibling feels entitled to certain items, so they take those items and tell everyone, "Mom said I could have that." In going through the estate, you may stumble upon the diamond ring everyone has been looking for years. Will you tell your siblings you found it or just quietly pocket it? It is not unusual for heirs to hide things so no one else can have them.

Also, there are heirs that will hire an appraiser behind the backs of the others to find out what has the most value in the estate. You may have a savvy sibling who knows more about what things are worth and takes a diamond bracelet you thought was costume jewelry. While the sibling may not think these actions involve trickery, they most certainly do, and the consequences among the children/heirs can be overwhelming.

The Caregivers

This is a broad and delicate subject. A caregiver can be hired by the family and loved deeply for the care and comfort they bring in a difficult situation. It is worth noting that most caregivers are incredible people, truly, angels among us.

But there are also caregivers out there who are planning to steal from your loved one. As with any occupation, you have some who are good and some who are bad.

All valuables need to be removed in a caregiver situation and placed in the hands of the Power of Attorney or executor for safekeeping, understanding this is a temporary transfer only. This scenario occurs both at home as well as in a facility. We have seen caregivers talk a demented patient into giving up their jewelry, etc.

Be extra aware if your loved one has memory impairment or Alzheimer's. Unfortunately, they are an easy target. Diamonds have been stolen right from the finger of a loved one who was napping or sedated. Other things in the house will disappear as well, including but not limited to electronics, cookware, DVDs, CDs.

Caregivers can be hired or they can be a family member. If a family member, this is a tremendous undertaking on their part and the others should realize the sacrifice being made to tend the loved one. It is not unusual for the family caregiver to receive an extra something special for taking care of mom and dad. It becomes the responsibility of the executor to recommend that. Other siblings may not agree, however, because that will take away from their share. Still, it is always a nice gesture to consider.

If the caregiver were a hired person, it is fine to offer them either something from the home or a money gift. If you offer something from the home, you choose the item for them. Again, we have seen caregivers use their keys and empty the entire home. Sometimes, a money gift is more appropriate.

Be prepared that a hired caregiver may approach you, saying, "Your mother promised she would take care of me," expecting money. If mom never mentioned this to you, it could be a line the caregiver is using to get something from the estate. Just be careful and use your gut instinct.

The Estranged Heir

Sometimes families just don't get along. A son or daughter may have left the home at an early age, never to return. Perhaps something happened in the family during childhood that caused a great rift. This relative could have had a falling out with someone in the family and, therefore, has strained relationships with the parents and/or siblings.

However, this relative is among the first to show up when it comes time to divide the personal belongings of a deceased parent; he insists on being given what he wants. Unless there is a will that specifically designates who gets what, this relative will generally be uncooperative and may even contest the division of assets.

The Greedy Heir

They don't call greed one of the deadly sins for no reason. Every family seems to have one person who wants everything, or at least the lion's share of the most valuable things; he or she can be aggressive in trying to obtain it all. This relative also tends to be a bit of a collector themselves and cares little about the parents' or siblings' wishes. This is the one who is the most unreasonable and uncooperative in dealings regarding the parents' estate and will most often challenge provisions of the will.

Logic and rules generally don't apply to them, but only to everyone around them. It does not matter if this person was close to the decedent or not. If they want an item, they are going to find a way to get it. Frequently, you will not be able to reason with this type of family member. Be sure this will become a highly volatile situation.

The "Entitled" Heir

Not to be confused with the greedy relative, the entitled relative is also alive and well in almost every family. This one can be recognized by how they say things: "I deserve it," "I've always wanted it," "Mom said I could have it," "I want it for my children," "I lived closest to mom and did everything for her and you live on the other side of the country and did nothing."

In some cases, the entitled child could be the least successful of everyone in the family; this is their way of trying to make it a more level playing field. They are trying to feel equally as important as their more successful siblings.

On the other hand, it can just as easily be the most successful child who desires mom's best possessions. At times, it becomes a scenario of "he said-she said," remembering mom or dad promised a certain child could have a special item. But as the years pass, the parent might forget and say the same thing to another child. This is why it is so important to document your wishes!

The Hasty Heir

In almost any estate where there are at least two siblings, more commonly a brother and a sister, it is not unusual that one will move slowly to go through everything and one will want the house cleaned out within the week. One might hire a dumpster, while the other is painstakingly going through every shred of paper, as a form of grieving.

However, it is not healthy for the house to sit for years, while everything in it continues to disintegrate; the same is true for things put in storage. Deal with stored belongings when you are sorting through the house.

This scenario can be compared to a Band-Aid. If you pull it off fast, the pain is only momentary. If you pull it off slowly, the pain inflicted can be great. Neither is optimal, but when it comes to estates, there needs to be a happy medium. If children clear out the home too fast and without professional guidance, hasty and "expensive" mistakes can occur.

I'll never forget the time I told a 50-yr. old male client not to put a thing in the dumpster until I arrived early the next morning. When I got there, the dumpster was half full! At the bottom, I spotted an antique Louis Vuitton trunk that was filled with WWI memorabilia. Fortunately, I was there to put a halt to this hasty action and sold those items for several thousand dollars.

The Feeling-Slighted Heir

When settling an estate, it is easy to feel slighted or taken advantage of for many reasons. One child/heir often feels like they did the majority of work while the loved one was still alive, as well as after death when dealing with the physical estate and the back-breaking work associated with it.

Some resentment is completely understandable. Another may feel that one sibling got more than they should have from the estate; they don't say anything about it, yet they harbor anger for decades to come.

Still another may be in a long distance situation and feel alienated from the whole process, thinking they will be cut out or that what they receive will be minimal because they are not near.

Be aware that most children, at one point or another, will feel slighted, and for the most part will resist this emotion by becoming more demanding than usual.

Section VI

How to Divide the Estate With the Family Intact

PREPARE FOR THIS DAY

Hopefully, you have not arrived at this page directly from the table of contents. Before the days of dividing the estate arrive, you need to understand the principles that guide this process. You need to understand and pledge to cooperate with the executor. You need to be aware of how we set values and expectations. Finally, you need to agree with the other heirs that there will be no fighting over things in the estate.

HIRE PROFESSIONAL ASSISTANCE

This is not a do-it-yourself project! Costly mistakes are often made by adult children who act in haste to get the task completed, like throwing things they shouldn't discard in dumpsters and sending valuables off to donation or trash.

☐ People often need legal advice. Don't get it from Cousin Sam who is a divorce attorney. Go to an estate planning attorney who knows the exact laws of the state in which the estate is located.

☐ Hire an objective appraiser to assign values, so items can be distributed as equitably as possible. Sometimes the family will reach an impasse and need help moving forward. It is the objective, yet skilled professional appraiser, who can move everyone forward again. By offering values on items or heirlooms that are in question, you will have a strong foundation on which to begin the equitable distribution process.

Remember that most arguments will erupt over the *perception that something is either extremely valuable or not valuable at all!* A personal property appraiser can bring all this to light with a formal written document, based on the reporting of truth and objective facts.

WHEN HIRING PROFESSIONALS, REMEMBER THE FOLLOWING:

☐ Always be sure to check with the Better Business Bureau whether the company you are hiring has any unresolved complaints against them. You can check them out online now. http://www.bbb.org/us/find-business-reviews

☐ How long have they been in business? How much experience do they have?

☐ Can they provide references and testimonials?

☐ Are they affiliated with any professional organizations? This will show if they are credible and serious about their work.

☐ Do they have a professional website? It's a must in this day and age.

☐ What is their fee structure and what does each service include?

☐ Are they insured and/or bonded?

☐ Have they presented a professionally written contract?

SETTING THE STAGE FOR THE DAY OF DIVISION

☐ **Communication** – It should be open but cautious, so you don't upset anyone.

☐ **Celebration** – Your loved one is gone and they certainly don't want the family fighting. Honor them by celebrating their life and the things they collected through life that brought them pleasure.

☐ **Music** – Have some calming music playing, preferably easy listening or classical.

☐ **Stories** – Share stories, especially funny stories, which may be connected to some of the items you are finding and dividing.

☐ **Food** – Bring some healthy food to nourish yourself through a long day: granola bars, trail mix, water or juice, breakfast or lunch sandwiches, fruit, or dark chocolate for an energy boost.

☐ **Photo** – Set up a framed photo of your loved one where heirs can see it, as if mom or dad is there with you watching you divide their belongings.

THE IMPORTANCE OF ORGANIZING, CLEANING, AND FINDING EVERYTHING

Organization is key. When you first walk into the estate after the last parent has died, you will think to yourself, "How on earth are we going to sort through this house and where do we begin?" You should purchase the companion volume to this guide which is all about cleaning out the estate: *A Boomer's Guide to Cleaning Out Your Parents' Estate in 30 Days or Less*, by Julie Hall.

☐ If you hire a personal property appraiser, they can at least direct you to the items that do have value, so that you can determine the division based upon wish lists and equitable distribution.

☐ Uncover all the items in the estate that have sentimental value. Hint: the waffle iron is probably not sentimental. This listing of sentimental items should not be long. Choose only the sentimental item(s) that really speak to you: dad's spectacles, mom's hairbrush, a letter from your favorite aunt, special family photographs. Keep it simple; understand that you cannot keep everything. It might be sentimental to you, but not to your children. Don't leave a mess for them; keep them in mind during the entire division process.

☐ If your loved one suffered from memory impairment or another affliction that had an impact on memory or organization, it is imperative that you leave no stone unturned. I can assure you that things are hiding in the estate: sometimes from paranoia, sometimes because of their Depression Era mindset, and sometimes because they simply don't remember where they hid it.

While it would be thrilling to find mom's diamond watch that no one has seen in years, it could very well be hiding or it may be gone. Your parent may have thrown some valuables away, or perhaps even given them away, and have no recollection of this.

If you check everywhere and do everything you can to be a detective in the home and outbuildings, you can at least breathe a little bit easier, knowing you did everything you could to find the valuables. Don't forget to look in purses and pockets!

☐ **Cleaning out is also very important**. Be sure to clear out the top shelf of the kitchen cabinet, or that dreadful closet that no one has opened in thirty years. You may find that treasured item; the one you always wondered where it ended up. Most of the time, you will find treasures hidden in the most bizarre places and further wonder what mom or dad were thinking when they placed them there.

Suggested places to search are attic rafters or basement crawl spaces, ice cube trays, inside or under a mattress. There are many more places to search for treasures and important paperwork, more than you would think of on your own. These are listed in the companion guide: *A Boomer's Guide to Cleaning Out Your Parents' Estate in 30 Days or Less* by Julie Hall.

☐ **When it doubt, hire a professional company that specializes in residential clean outs**. They will sort through everything and report back to you their findings, and whether anything of value was discovered. Sometimes the task is just too overwhelming and professional help is both wanted and needed.

Section VII

The Top 12 Practical Problems and Solutions

PROBLEM #1: When you want to keep everything

SOLUTION: Your house is full of stuff also, so take photographs to remember things. Learn to let go, and realize this stuff will be a burden on your children at some point. If you don't let go for yourself, then do it for them.

Understand the chances are very good your children and grandchildren do not want to keep what you would choose for them as heirlooms or future keepsakes. Their generation is not nearly as sentimental and would prefer cash to anything else the majority of the time.

Even if you try to project what they would like to have when they become young adults, proceed with caution. As they become adults and you hand them grandma's china, they will look at you as if you are from another planet. Most would rather go to IKEA. Most would rather have the cash.

Remember that no material possession is worth losing or destroying a family relationship. Ultimately, you can't take it with you either.

PROBLEM #2: When the heirs are a long distance from the estate

SOLUTION: The optimal solution would be to find resources in advance and plan together with your parents before they are gone. Get to know their local clergy, health care professionals, attorney, financial planner, and accountant. Also, you should learn where all of mom and dad's assets and documents are located, as well as all the professionals they work with.

Research where to find an estate liquidator at http://www.ASELonline.com. Locate a personal property appraiser through a local estate planning attorney's office. Find out from the county on what day the garbage comes to pick up, and find the location of the closest recycle center. Also find local charities to drop off donations. If possible, prepare all this information ahead of the crisis.

PROBLEM #3: When you suspect that your parent(s) had hidden stashes or placed valuables in hiding places

SOLUTION: There are countless stories of someone buying a piece of furniture in an estate sale only to find a hidden treasure in the drawer or taped to the bottom. Valuable papers have been found hidden behind a piece of framed artwork.

Be sure to ask your parents and loved ones ahead of time if there are any known stashes in the house or on the grounds (gold coins, jewelry, cash, stock certificates, etc). Typically distrustful of banks, this was the generation that hid their valuables and cash on the premises.

Anything could be hidden anywhere, especially if memory impairment is involved. Leave no stone unturned and look anywhere you can think of that is "out of the ordinary."

PROBLEM #4: When some of the personal property is missing and not available to divide equally

SOLUTION: If there are assets that have already been taken or removed from the home, the value of those assets needs to be included in the final accounting and division tally. Accounting for property already taken is absolutely necessary to promote fairness and prevent siblings/heirs from getting really upset. If the items were given while your loved one was alive, or if an item was specifically bequeathed in the will, those things should remain with the new owner and should not be counted in the final tally.

The difficulty lies in determining whether an item was intentionally given away in life. It may simply have been taken but excuses are made. Only you can be the judge of that.

However, if these items were just taken because a sibling felt like taking them or felt entitled to them without the permission of the executor or others, request that the items should be returned until such a time as they are properly distributed. There is, unfortunately, always that chance that whoever took the items will never 'fess up and never return the item.

Here's another reason why it is so important for the executor to retrieve keys and change the locks. It is also equally important for the loved one to be in control when they gift items prior to death; they should then tell all involved "I gave Jane the mantle clock, Sue the antique lamp, Bill the old fishing rods, etc." When everyone is on the same page, the process goes much smoother.

PROBLEM #5: When more than one heir wants the same thing

SOLUTION: In the common scenario, one or more of the siblings will want the same item. Depending on what is the item, there are several different ways to diffuse this challenge. These solutions require the assistance of the heirs who are in this headlock. Whoever is involved needs to listen and do their best to cooperate. If they remain in a permanent tug-of-war, the solutions provided will not work, no matter how good or sound.

Scenario A: If something is dividable, should we divide it and put it behind us?

Solution A: If you have a dividable item, for example, a china set or flatware service, the King Solomon approach can work. You can divide equitably because you have multiple pieces involved.

However, it is important to realize that, from the perspective of an appraiser or estate expert, this scenario will eventually hurt the value of that set. People want entire sets, not partial sets. If the items were ever to be sold, which your children might do one day, the partial set will not have the value of the entire set. Everyday, we find these partial sets in estates along with the story that they were all divided to keep the peace. While this is an option, think about it carefully.

Scenario B: We have a document that certain people (in-laws, friends, neighbors, charity, etc.) get certain things. Do we just give those items to them, or divide those items among ourselves?

Solution B: If a written document specifies a certain heir or friend to receive a special item(s), it should be done according to the wishes of the loved one. However, you may want to exercise caution. It is not unusual for a maid, caregiver, neighbor, friend, even a family member, to say things like, "Your mother always said I could have that painting because I have admired it for 35 years." Or, "Your mom said she would take care of me financially after she died."

While mom or dad may have said these things (and just as equally may NOT have said these things), you must take into consideration what mom shared with you, what she wrote, if she really wanted this person to have a particular item, or, if that person is spinning a tale. People will often try to pull the wool over your eyes, so it is recommended that the heirs discuss this together before giving anything away. You may not have any proof that mom told the maid she would giver her $10,000, but you can offer her a gift if you would like, as a gesture of your appreciation.

It is the executor's responsibility to make sure everything required of him/her by the state has been fulfilled, before distributing anything. When in doubt, hire an estate planning attorney for assistance.

Scenario C: Two of my siblings are fighting over a single heirloom. How do you split that?

Solution C: This is very common. When two or more are arguing over the same item(s), you have a few options, but ultimately the level of stubbornness of those individuals will determine the resolution.

- One heir simply "turns the other cheek" and forfeits the item to the other. Remember that all of the values need to be kept equitable. If Sue gets a $5,000 item and Barbara gets a $200 item, that is not equitable and other arrangements must be made, whether in cash assets or other items, to make up for the $4,800 deficit.

- On sibling can offer to buy the item from the others and take it out of their inheritance.

- They can write up an agreement and share the item, if it is small enough to share. Then again, this decision only postpones that inevitable decision for later in life. When the siblings die, now their children have to contend with the same item.

- If no one can agree and the arguing continues in a "no one is going to give in" pattern, I recommend the executor *sell the item* through an appropriate auction and split the proceeds by the number of siblings. In this case, the King Solomon approach doesn't work if it is a single item, like a Civil War sword, a grandfather clock, family bible, or diamond ring. Of course the siblings will be upset, but that is more acceptable than resenting each other the remainder of their lives.

- What would mom or dad want? Would they permit this kind of treatment towards one another? In most cases, the answer is no. They would be disappointed, having trusted you to make decisions that they probably should have made while they were alive; for whatever reason, they didn't. You can't go back; you can only go forwards. So go forward, realizing what your parents would have wanted. Go forth, doing what they would have wanted.

PROBLEM # 6: When one person wants the lion's share

I had a client who hired me because he knew his daughter would be problematic when he passed away. He knew that she would want it all and walk all over the other siblings; he wanted to prevent that while he was still alive. His own words were, "She will want the lion's share and I want to prevent that before my time comes." What he requested was exactly what I usually recommend:

SOLUTION: Prior to death, this solution is optimal. Yet after a loved one dies, it is absolutely necessary to have an appraiser ascertain what has value and what doesn't. Once an appraisal report was written, the father mentioned in the above story placed one copy of that appraisal with his other legal papers so when his time came, the executor (who had the other copy) would know how to proceed with equitable distribution.

Certainly values can change over time, depending on a multitude of different factors. If it has been five years or more since that appraisal was written, hire the appraiser back for an update.

It is imperative that if the will says everything is to be split equitably among the heirs, then no one can get the lion's share. The executor must take the responsibility to make this happen.

PROBLEM # 7: When you uncover a valuable treasure and the treasure is on someone's wish list

Recently one of my clients requested that I attend a family meeting as they divided mom's jewelry. Several of the pieces were already spoken for, as mom (prior to her death), had given them away to her daughters, one son and a daughter-in-law. Looking at all the jewelry that was on the table, I spotted one ring with a purplish stone that was given to the daughter-in-law by mom, prior to her death.

No one thought anything of it; they thought it was just an inexpensive amethyst. It wasn't an amethyst. It was an exceptionally large and valuable Alexandrite. Once we sent it to an expert and had it identified as an Alexandrite and knew the value, which was very significant, suddenly all the children turned on the daughter-in-law.

This daughter-in-law felt that since mom gave it to her, it belonged to her. It had been her gift. The biological children argued that mom didn't know how valuable it really was. Both of them were right in their own way. As you can see, we had a total impasse.

SOLUTION: They looked to me for advice and I could only think of three possible outcomes.

- Sell it and divide the proceeds.
- Keep it and deal with the bad feelings the remainder of their lives.

- (Addressing the daughter-in-law) Why not sell the ring and bring all of mom's children and their spouses on a cruise?

What happened? She sold the ring and took everyone on a wonderful trip. Because of her ability to assess this challenge and because she didn't want family tensions to continue, she instead chose to foster happy feelings among the heirs. Also, she probably would have earned the respect and admiration of her mother-in-law who had recently passed away. She took the high road and made everyone happy.

PROBLEM # 8: When you find a treasure and no one else knows you found it

You finally found mom's diamond earrings which no one has seen in 20 years. You just happened to find them in one of mom's old coat pockets. You've always wanted them, but so has your sister. What do you do?

It is true that honesty is the best policy. Sooner or later, someone will find out or come to know about it. Things like this always have a way of coming to light. When someone finds out, it is going to be an ugly situation.

SOLUTION: The correct thing to do is give it to the executor who has a responsibility to do the right thing on behalf of the estate. Disclose that you found them and would like to have them placed on your wish list. Your sister might also place them on her wish list and "finder's keepers" is not a guarantee that you are now the rightful new owner.

The same is true if you happen to notice things are missing from the estate, or you see someone pocket an item. Always report back to the executor. Personally, I always suggest taking the high road. Even the best of people, especially those going through the grief process, can become dishonest, feel they are entitled, or suddenly demonstrate greed. If you keep the item, will you be able to live with that decision?

From the very beginning, it is important to create an atmosphere of trust. By doing this, cooperation usually follows. However, if a sibling feels they have been cheated or taken advantage of, the gloves come off and the fighting begins.

PROBLEM # 9: When one sibling involves grandchildren immediately, or wants extra "picks" or selections for their own children

This type of heir will attempt to use the grandchildren to justify additional picks, on top of their own selections, "to remember grandma by", and to have these sentimental heirlooms for their children (the grandchildren of the decedent).

Meanwhile, their children may or may not have been close to grandma; they certainly don't need a bunch of things in order to remember grandma. Likely, they don't truly want much, and this is what most Boomer children need to recognize. Ask your children if there is anything of grandma's which they want. You'll find that most of them do not want much, maybe a couple of small items. A favorite photo and a couple of small items are thoughtful and special; keep it simple for you and for them.

SOLUTION: Remember, siblings are always the first tier in selecting items, unless the will specifies differently or the decedent does not have a will. Grandchildren are certainly important, but when it comes to the division of property, immediate heirs are primary. If a sibling feels strongly about their children (grandchildren) having items from the estate, it must be this way:

1) After the siblings or immediate children conduct their division of property

2) Use their own personal selections for the grandchildren and forfeit some of their own desires

3) Politely request from the estate that they would like to have these items for the grandchildren after the siblings choose, and will pay for them out of their personal inheritance.

While this last solution may seem rather business-like, it is for a reason. All the siblings want is *what is fair*; what they *perceive* as fair. Unfortunately, everyone has their own idea of what is fair. If you take and take, or even give the perception of being a taker, this isn't fair.

If you buy from the estate, at least the monies will go into the estate pot and be divided, but everyone has to agree with these terms. You need to discuss this with the executor first and then include the others, so everyone is in agreement. Hard feelings come from being left out and not kept up on what is happening during the process.

4) No double dipping. It is not appropriate to choose something for yourself and then let your children also choose, ahead of your siblings. This is an exceptionally painful and abrupt endeavor which should not be permitted.

PROBLEM #10: When extended family gets in the way

It may be your aunt, a close friend from church, a long lost grandson who was just released from prison, or a greedy niece. It doesn't matter; there always seems to be one person that gets in the way, either intentionally or unintentionally.

This is where the executor plays an important role. His/her job is to protect the assets and fulfill the responsibilities to the decedent. It is up to the executor to keep the extended family and friends at bay until all the decisions have been made. Many unpleasant events will transpire, often because the executor is uncertain how to contain the extended family member.

SOLUTION: Open and firm communication is recommended with everyone involved and particularly with the person causing the difficulties.

- "At this time, we all have to wait until we go through the probate process."
- "Immediate family wishes are addressed first. Depending on what's left over, the extended family may be able to have a couple of pieces, but her children come first."
- "No decisions will be made until 'A, B, and C' happens. It's a lengthy process."

- "When the decisions are made you will be notified."
- "Thank you for your interest and care but at this time....."
- "I will call you if we need your help; thank you."
- "Nothing is to be distributed until we've had an appraiser and other professionals come in."
- "I know mom was very important to you. The piece you would like to have is going to my sister. After all the children have made their selections, I will let you know."

PROBLEM # 11: When neighbors or friends expect to get something from the estate

As with anything in life, you get the good and you get the bad. The same holds true for neighbors and friends. In virtually every estate I have personally been involved in, I have successfully predicted that a neighbor or long time friend will attempt to:

1) take more than the family wants to give,
2) attempt to help themselves (because they have a key they shouldn't have),
3) offer assistance in order to get a closer look at the estate items, or
4) claim that the decedent wanted them to have a specific item.

It is difficult to predict behavior even in people you have known your entire life. Just when you know they are gentle-spirited and generous, they show you a whole new color that is far less attractive. Just be aware and be protective.

Families often complain that a neighbor comes by during the week of the funeral or the week they are clearing out the house and says, "Oh, your mom promised I could have that." Naturally the children want to honor mom's wishes, but if mom never said that, or your gut is telling you this is not the truth, listen to your instinct.

SOLUTION: What should you say in this situation? "Sally, you have been such a good friend and neighbor to mom and we are all so grateful. Unfortunately, we have so much going on at the moment and the family has yet to make those important decisions. So until we do, I'm afraid we need to leave everything just as it is, until the siblings all get together. They get first choice; I am sure you understand."

As a nice gesture, you and your siblings can also gift something else to the neighbor, especially if you never heard mom mention that certain piece should go to this woman. This is not the time to be shy!

PROBLEM # 12: To store or not to store...

Some siblings want everything to be over quickly, and either feel too overwhelmed with the amount of stuff, or don't have enough space for what they want to keep from the estate, so they turn to storage as a solution. At best, it is a temporary answer but definitely not a long term solution.

☐ Storage is a place where we tend to forget the contents; storage companies are banking on that. You know the old saying, "Out of sight, out of mind."

☐ While these items are sitting in storage because they have been temporarily forgotten or undecided upon, the monthly bills keep coming. That can add up to a substantial amount of expense for the estate to pay.

☐ Often, but not always, people will keep items in storage for long periods of time because they feel the items have value or will increase in value. Furniture, in general, doesn't do very well stored in an environment that is not the same climate as your home. Items can be stacked or not placed in storage correctly, causing damage.

By the time I see some of the stored items, they have lost some value due to damage (heat, cold, humidity, mildew, mold, veneer coming off, plus numerous other issues).

☐ What most people finally realize is that the items they are keeping in storage are of less value than what it is costing them to rent the space. These are all important things to consider.

☐ You believe that your adult children or grandchildren might want these things so you store them. Chances are they don't. Statistically, the younger generations have little to no appreciation for grandmother's things. They don't want the 65 year old sofa or dark mahogany furniture. They want IKEA, Pottery Barn, and cold hard cash.

SOLUTION: We simply have too much stuff. If you don't have enough space in your home, look to downsize your possessions so you can make room for some of these preferred belongings.

Think long and hard before "saving a bunch of things" for subsequent generations. Their lives and style choices are simple and contemporary. Some grandchildren might show an interest in grandpa's fishing equipment or grandma's jewelry, but more often than not, they don't care for crystal, silver (polishing the silver is labor intensive), china, or old furniture. Carefully consider before storing and saving things for years; you may discover no one wants these things.

If you save all of this for your children, plus all the things you have in your home, you will be leaving a tremendous burden to your own children, who don't want to deal with this burden. Generally, the younger the generation, the less attached they seem to be to things.

Section VIII

Gifting: How to Avoid Distribution Problems Before Death

IN THE IDEAL WORLD, DECIDE WHO GETS WHAT BEFORE DEATH HAPPENS

☐ Children, the optimal solution is to talk with your parents before mental decline or death.

☐ Get your own, and your parent's, legal documents in order. It is worth every penny of the cost to sit down with an estate planning attorney, so you can discuss your situation and future wishes for yourself and your heirs.

☐ Discuss the children's wants, and decide who gets what.

☐ Discuss gifting prior to death to minimize fighting. Parents can either physically distribute while alive or create a master list that is given to all heirs.

☐ Have these gifts/heirlooms appraised before distribution.

☐ Consider gifting prior to death to see joy on recipient's face, thin out your estate, and minimize future fighting among heirs.

☐ Boomers, remember to do this for your kids too!

Section IX

Family Challenges and Solutions

Dodge Relational Minefields

Children Who Were Caregivers

Being the child who is a caregiver is a difficult situation, because sometimes the will specifies more to go to the caregiver child, and sometimes, it's the complete opposite. In the event you have a sibling or close family member that was a caregiver, you must realize the sacrifices that they made for your loved one. There's nothing easy about care giving!

Some siblings get very upset if more is left to the caregiver sibling, as they feel there should be an equitable distribution. If the caregiver was left out of the will, or didn't get as much from the estate as the others, that seems unfair also. Siblings will sometimes complain that the care giving sister had free room and board.

The outcome of this challenge depends on what the will specifies. Possibly, the will was never updated to reflect the current infirmity and care in the loved one's life.

If you feel your caregiver sibling should be given more, that is a very nice gesture. This should be arranged with the executor to offer cash assets or another asset, but all siblings should agree, unless this is already stated in the will.

There are countless scenarios surrounding a caregiver situation; each one is very different. Use your instinct, but also be compassionate about this tender issue.

Blended Families

There are more blended families today than ever before. It is worth some thought that our parents' generation didn't have to deal with this challenge very much. During their youth, there weren't many divorces and remarriages.

As a result, you will face some unique situations as you deal with the loss of your parents. If this describes your situation, I don't need to tell you that the blessings of a blended family, as a result of divorce or the death of a parent, also bring some awkward and uncomfortable issues.

For example, if you have a stepbrother or stepsister from a second marriage, should either of them be included in the distribution of heirlooms or wealth? Will the second spouse receive the bulk of the estate over the blood children? All of this depends on the clarity of the will and estate planning between the parents and stepparents. Here's another vital reason to have all of your legal affairs in order.

In general terms, you treat the distribution of property the same way you would if your family was not blended. Try to get your parents to see the importance of this issue and make these decisions early, and not leave it up to you and your siblings to figure out.

Make sure your parents update their will when they remarry. Prepare as much as you can ahead of time. Wills are of vast importance in all scenarios, but blended family situations can turn ugly, especially when there is no will. I strongly encourage you to speak with an estate planning attorney to get all the specifics about blended families.

I remember the time a client remarried after being widowed. He died shortly after they got married and did not have a will. In his state, the new wife got half of his estate, and his blood children got the other half. The children were not happy!

Here is a typical scenario of an older parent who gets divorced or remarries after a spouse dies. Often as they age, they begin to think about how they want to divide their property. The problem is their blended family may already be fighting over the heirlooms. The parent doesn't know what to do, so they don't do anything at all, because they don't want to cause further aggravation.

Any heirloom that was a part of the first marriage should go only to the children from that marriage. In this case, the man's wife was also previously married. My advice was that anything from her side of the family should go to her biological children only. This, at least, will keep it simple.

Distribution of these items should take place while the parents are still living to avoid future feuding among stepchildren.

The Only Child

The good news is you don't have anyone to really fight with, except maybe an extended family member. The bad news is you are going to need more help. If you have cousins, nieces, or nephews that want to pitch in, especially if you pay them a little gas or pizza money on the side, that's a great way to enlist their help.

Become the master of delegation and enlist the help of close friends. If you are not familiar with the area where your parents lived, a local college will have students looking for work, or your parent's church or synagogue may have volunteers. Ask around and you will soon find the assistance you need. Know the plan and know the local resources in your parent's area.

No Children

When there are no children involved, things can still get complicated. Therefore, it is important to select an executor that you trust, so he/she can be prepared to meet the challenges of dealing with an estate with no help. Just like the only child listed above, trusted local resources are going to be needed. Finding them in advance will help ensure the estate will be handled in a timely manner.

In cases with no children, many leave their assets to extended relatives, charities, professional organizations, their religious affiliation, etc. The executor will be responsible to have the assets distributed according to the specifications of the will.

In-Laws (or Outlaws?)

Here's a taboo subject among families! They all think about it in the back of their minds, but few ever open a discussion about it. A family meeting is the perfect time for the executor to discuss the plan of action and what he/she feels should take place. It is also a good time for the executor to hear suggestions from the heirs.

Many families have shared with me over the years that they are concerned with an in-law who will over-step their bounds. Even if the in-law was close to your loved one, it is best that the division and selection process take place only among the immediate children. If the loved one has included the in-law in the will, and left them a special item, make sure that item is given to them. Yet in-laws should respectfully remain in the background.

It is common and contentious enough for the siblings to quarrel or bicker, but when an in-law steps into the picture, and steps on toes, the fighting will escalate at a rapid rate. It is best to avoid the fighting altogether and never even step into the ring.

Unscrupulous Heirs

You've heard the stories: changing locks late at night, sneaking in when no one is near the estate to help themselves to the good stuff, removing items so the other heirs never have a chance, throwing a diamond bracelet in a box with costume jewelry claiming it was just junk jewelry, the in-town kids take first dibs and the out-of-town heirs get the leftovers, an heir destroying a document important to the estate.

It is not easy to predict some of these shocking behaviors that you never expected to see in a family member who has, for the most part, always been calm and on the level. Just when you least expect it, they have changed before your very eyes and you don't recognize the person in front of you. This is more common than you know.

However, if you look closely and pay attention, you will see the clues that things are getting ready to get shaken up a bit:

☐ Things begin disappearing ~ small, insignificant things at first - then more and more items that cannot be found and no one is talking.

☐ You begin to notice an "entitlement mentality"

☐ They start talking about how their children want this, that, and the other thing, which may or may not be true.

☐ A sibling/heir might request from the loved one in advance what they would like to have, unknown to the others.

☐ They go into the estate and start "cleaning it out" to spare the others and be helpful.

☐ Excessive questions about finances, values, etc.

☐ False claims: "She promised that to me."

☐ Questions about when people would be on premises in hopes of gaining exclusive access.

☐ A previous history of unscrupulous behavior

☐ Family members down on their luck

☐ Those that can rationalize this kind of behavior: "They don't need this. They have plenty of money."

☐ Retaining their own lawyer

☐ Loitering around a certain item(s), marking their territory

☐ Accusatory tendencies: they take things and then blame another

☐ They stop talking to other family members

Estranged Heirs

It's never easy on anyone when a long lost family member comes back, especially when it is surrounding an illness or death. Sometimes they come back because they feel badly and wish to make amends. Sometimes they feel guilty and are looking for a way to ease the guilt. Sometimes they have no feelings at all and simply want to take their share of the assets and then leave.

This is a sticky issue because the siblings usually have strong feelings about the one who left and never looked back. They weren't there to call and comfort, or they were never available to help out. There are even times when people just aren't capable of tending to a family member who is very ill; they can't stomach it and the family feels they took the easy way out.

Whatever the reason for the estrangement, if it isn't healed by the time the loved one died, it never will be and the wounds of everyone involved will always be raw. These relationships become extremely strained. They become even more so when the estranged one returns with open hands, wanting their share.

It all depends on what the will stipulates. If they get equal share, that's the answer, like it or not. If there is no will, the state will step in and divide the property in ways you probably won't approve of anyway. That's another important reason to have a will or trust.

Regardless of how you feel about this person, find out the reason they came back and then formulate your opinion. Sometimes it is best to look the other way. In most cases, though, the estranged one continues being estranged long after the parent dies because most of the time, the other children walk away and choose not to heal that wound. There is no win-win here, unless all involved make a special effort to heal the situation.

Section X

Conclusion:
Looking Forward

Hopefully, you have completed the division of your parent's estate and heirlooms, using this book as your guide. You are still on speaking terms with your siblings, and the executor has settled the estate. While you still grieve the loss of your loved one, you enjoy your memories and the heirlooms you received.

WHAT NOW?

☐ Take proactive steps now to prepare your own family for your inevitable infirmity or death.

☐ Don't assume you can wait because your children are young, or you have no children. The length of our lives is not guaranteed.

☐ Keep control of your possessions; don't let them control you. Try to reduce the "stuff" around you by donating to charity, etc. Remember, we only use about 20% of what we own.

☐ If one parent is still living, have the necessary conversations with them. Be sure they have their important documents prepared, updated if necessary, and you know where they are kept.

☐ Make sure you have prepared an updated will and your family knows where it is kept.

☐ Assign a trusted family member or friend to serve as the executor of your estate. It is usually not wise to appoint as executor one of the children who will gain from the distribution of your possessions.

☐ Create a basic spreadsheet of your possessions with each child's name beside the items you have chosen for them.

☐ Of all the things you might leave behind, the most valuable gift you can give your family is harmony.

By taking time right now to plan for the future, you will help your children avoid the fighting that has become so common in my business, and give yourself peace of mind as well.

Section XI

Helpful Resource Links

The Internet is a great place to look for help with specific issues relating to caring for your aging parents and liquidating their estate. Here's a list of places to start.

APPRAISALS

www.appraisers.org
American Society of Appraisers

www.isa-appraisers.org
International Society of Appraisers

DISPOSAL / RECYCLE

www.shredit.com
Shredding service

www.recycle.net
Help and resources for getting rid of junk

ELDER CARE SUPPORT

www.aarp.org
National website for the American Association of Retired Persons that provides education, advocacy, and research

www.aarp.org/drive
AARP Driver Safety Program
To locate a refresher driving program in your area

www.agenet.com
Information for the elderly, including financial, legal, health care, and other advice

www.Aging-Parents-and-Elder-Care.com
Aging Solutions — Articles, comprehensive checklists, and links to key resources designed to make it easier for people caring for an aging parent or elderly spouse to quickly find the information they need

NOTES:

_____
_____
_____
_____
_____
_____
_____
_____
_____
_____
_____
_____
_____
_____
_____
_____
_____
_____
_____
_____
_____
_____
_____
_____
_____
_____

www.aahsa.org   202-783-2242
American Association of Homes and Services for the Aging (AAHSA)

www.alfa.org   703-894-1805
Assisted Living Federation of America
Consumer information on elder housing options, services, and protections

www.agingcare.com
Resources about aging and elder care, ranging from support with daily living to financial and legal information as well as community support.

www.caregiverslibrary.org
National Caregivers Library

www.familycaregivers.org
Center for Family Caregivers

www.caps4caregivers.org   800-227-7294
Children of Aging Parents
Information, resources, and referrals for caregivers of aging parents.

Eldercare Locator   800-677-1116
The Eldercare Locator can put you in contact with the Office for the Aging in your area, which provides help in locating needed services in your area (a service administered by the National Association of Area Agencies on Aging and the National Association of State Units on Aging).

National Transit Resource Center   800-527-8279
Provides referrals for transportation for seniors

www.ec-online.net
Eldercare Online
Whether you are caring for a spouse, parent, relative, or neighbor, this is an online community where supportive peers and professionals help you improve quality of life for yourself and your elder.

NOTES:

_____
_____
_____
_____
_____
_____
_____
_____
_____
_____
_____
_____
_____
_____
_____
_____
_____
_____
_____
_____
_____
_____
_____

www.extendedcare.com/Search/Search.aspx
Extended Care Info Network
Detailed directory of long-term care providers, home
health agencies, retirement communities, hospices,
and nursing homes; searchable by city, county, state,
type of facility, or institution name; also lists related
Internet resources.

www.caregiving.org
National Alliance for Caregiving
Offering information, education, and support to
families caring for loved ones.

www.4fate.org
Foundation Aiding the Elderly ~ Assuring our elders
are treated with care, dignity, and the utmost respect
during their final years when they can no longer take
care of themselves

www.hospicefoundation.org   800-854-3402
Hospice Foundation of America
Information on Medicare, managed care, Medigap
insurance, long-term care insurance, long-term care
facilities, and reports on health care fraud prevention
programs

ELDER HEALTHCARE ISSUES

www.alz.org   800-272-3900
Alzheimer's Association

www.alzinfo.org
Comprehensive information about Alzheimer's
disease

www.heart.org   800-242-8721
American Heart Association
Information on heart disease as well as local chapter
information

www.cancer.org   800-227-2345
American Cancer Society

NOTES:
_____
_____
_____
_____
_____
_____
_____
_____
_____
_____
_____
_____
_____
_____
_____
_____
_____
_____
_____
_____
_____
_____
_____
_____
_____

www.strokeassociation.org   888-478-7653
American Stroke Association

www.BenefitsCheckUp.org
A free, easy-to-use service that identifies federal and state assistance programs for older Americans

www.kff.org   202-347-5270
Kaiser Family Foundation
Talking with your parents about Medicare and health coverage

www.webmd.com
General medical site with definitions of medical terms and information on diseases and available treatments

www.wellspouse.org   800-838-0879
Well Spouse Foundation
Support and resources for spousal caregivers

www.nadsa.org   877-745-1440
National Adult Day Services Association (NADSA)

www.nahc.org   202-547-7424
National Association for Home Care & Hospice
Advises on selecting a home care or hospice provider and locates agencies in the area

www.caremanager.org
National Association of Professional Geriatric Care Managers

www.ncal.org   202-842-4444
National Center for Assisted Living
Information on all aspects of assisted living and residential care facilities

NOTES:

_____
_____
_____
_____
_____
_____
_____
_____
_____
_____
_____
_____
_____
_____
_____
_____
_____
_____
_____
_____
_____
_____
_____
_____
_____

www.theconsumervoice.org   202-332-2275
National Consumer Voice for Quality Long-Term Care

www.talkaboutrx.org   301-340-3940
National Council on Patient Information and Education
Questions to ask when taking prescription and nonprescription medicines safe medicine use.

www.ncoa.org   202-479-1200
National Council on the Aging
Organizations and professionals dedicated to promoting the dignity, self-determination, and well-being of older persons

www.nfcacares.org   800-896-3650
National Family Caregivers Association (NFCA)

www.health.nih.gov   301-496-4000
National Institutes of Health – Seniors Health

www.nmha.org   800-969-6642
Mental Health America
Free information about mental health, mental illness, and local treatment facilities

www.parkinson.org   800-473-4636
National Parkinson Foundation
Free information, support, and local resources

www.nhcoa.org   202-347-9733
National Hispanic Council on Aging

ESTATE LIQUIDATION

www.aselonline.com
American Society of Estate Liquidators

www.auctioneers.org
National Association of Auctioneers

NOTES:

_____
_____
_____
_____
_____
_____
_____
_____
_____
_____
_____
_____
_____
_____
_____
_____
_____
_____
_____
_____
_____
_____
_____
_____

FINANCIAL

www.fpanet.org
Financial Planners Association

www.centerltc.org
Center for LTC Financing
Long term care financing information, assistance, and reform.

GOVERNMENT

www.aoa.gov   202-619-0724
U.S. Administration on Aging
Elder care ideas, topics, elder abuse, LTC ombudsman.

www.seniors.gov   800-333-4636
Firstgov - Access to government websites and information

www.medicare.gov   800-633-4227
U.S. government site for Medicare information, including comparison of health and drug plans

www.medicare.gov/Nhcompare/Home.asp
Medicare Nursing Home Ratings
A tool that enables you to read about ratings of local nursing homes in your area

www.hhs.gov   877-696-6775
U.S. Department of Health and Human Services
Agency for protecting the health of U.S. residents

www.ncea.aoa.gov
U.S. Administration on Aging's National Center on Elder Abuse

www.ssa.gov   800-772-1213
U.S. Social Security Administration online information and resources

NOTES:

_____

_____

_____

_____

_____

_____

_____

_____

_____

_____

_____

_____

_____

_____

_____

_____

_____

_____

_____

_____

_____

_____

_____

LEGAL ASSISTANCE

www.search-attorneys.com
To find an estate planning, probate, or elder law attorney

www.naela.org
National Academy of Elder Law Attorneys

www.abanet.org/aging/toolkit   202-662-1000
American Bar Association Commission on Law and Aging
Consumer's Tool Kit for Health Care Advance Planning

www.bbb.org/us/consumers
Better Business Bureau Foundation
Provides information about consumer frauds and scams, and tips for prevention

www.preventelderabuse.com
National Committee for the Prevention of Elder Abuse ~ Committed to help fight any abuse, and working to educate the public about the misuse of guardianships imposed on elders

www.ethicalwill.com
Information on creating an ethical will

ORGANIZING

www.optoutprescreen.com   888-567-8688
Stop unwanted junk mail

www.napo.net
National Association of Professional Organizers

www.elderweb.com
Locating records and property

www.nasmm.org
National Association of Senior Move Managers

NOTES:
_____
_____
_____
_____
_____
_____
_____
_____
_____
_____
_____
_____
_____
_____
_____
_____
_____
_____
_____
_____
_____
_____
_____
_____
_____

Section XII

Worksheets and Forms

➢ Sample Letter from Executor to Heirs

➢ Wish List Spreadsheet (Example)

➢ Wish List Spreadsheet (Blank)

SAMPLE LETTER FROM EXECUTOR TO HEIRS

November 30, 2010

Re: Update on Mom's estate and the division of personal property

Dear _____, _____, _____, _____,

Realizing this has been a difficult time for all of us, I just wanted to keep you all posted on the lengthy and detailed process of handling mom's estate. It is moving forward, but your patience is needed and greatly appreciated.

The division of her personal items and heirlooms will take place as soon as I get approval from the attorney. But before that can take place, I have decided the best way to proceed would be to call in an objective third party, a personal property appraiser, to help ascertain what has value and what doesn't. That will ensure that the division of property will be equitable to each of us, and that is what mom wanted in her will.

It would be very helpful if each of the <u>immediate siblings only</u> could fill out a wish list (see attached) of the items *they would like to have* from the estate. This wish list is not a guarantee you will receive these items. All of these desired items will be professionally appraised and those values will be placed on each individual wish list to compare the final totals. For those who are not interested in much of personal property, other assets or cash will be used to make it equitable.

There is nothing easy about dividing an estate. While it is normal for tensions and emotions to be higher than usual during this time, we must all agree to do everything in our power to get along, be kind and not fight. If we run into a problem, we will find a solution, but it will take all of us working together to make that happen.

Thank you in advance for thinking about these issues and I will be back in touch with you as soon as I know further information.

Appreciatively,

Wish List Spreadsheet (Example)
(hypothetical appraised values)

PERSON	ITEM	APPRAISED VALUE	DUPLICATE WISHES?	WITH WHOM?
Karen	Mantel clock	$200	No	
	Silver bell collection	$250	No	
	Painting in Mom's room	$375	No	
	Painting in spare room	$175	No	
	Rooster statue in kitchen	$25	No	
	Mom's perfume bottles	$150	No	
	Antique school desk	$35	No	
	Mom's childhood doll	$75	No	
	Grandma's wedding quilt	$375	No	
	Sterling silver flatware	$1,700	No	
	Centerpiece in dining room	$45	No	
	Gold curio cabinet in living room	$225	No	
	Chandelier, crystal and brass	$1,500	Yes	Jimmy
	Grandfather's tall case clock	$9,000	Yes	Jimmy
	Four-gallon pottery churn	$175	No	
	Mom's diamond earrings	$850	No	
	Antique fireplace screen	$695	Yes	Jimmy
	Dining room table and chairs	$1,000	Yes	Jimmy
	Karen's TOTAL	$16,850		

PERSON	ITEM	APPRAISED VALUE	DUPLICATE WISHES?	WITH WHOM?
Jimmy	Grandfather's pocket watch	$175	No	
	Power tools in garage	$250	No	
	Grandfather's oak roll top desk	$1,200	No	
	Dad's pipe collection on stand	$55	No	
	Dad's letter opener	$15	No	
	Dining room table and chairs	$1,000	Yes	Karen
	La-Z-Boy chair in den	$250	No	
	Bronze eagle statue on Dad's desk	$375	No	
	John Deere garden tractor	$2,100	No	
	Chandelier, crystal and brass	$1,500	Yes	Karen
	Grandfather's tall case clock	$9,000	Yes	Karen
	Antique fireplace screen	$695	Yes	Karen
	Jimmy's TOTAL	$16,615		

Wish List Spreadsheet
(Make as many copies as necessary)

PERSON	ITEM	APPRAISED VALUE	DUPLICATE WISHES?	WITH WHOM?

Wish List Spreadsheet
(Make as many copies as necessary)

PERSON	ITEM	APPRAISED VALUE	DUPLICATE WISHES?	WITH WHOM?

NOTES:

NOTES:

NOTES:

www.ingramcontent.com/pod-product-compliance
Lightning Source LLC
LaVergne TN
LVHW081319060426
835509LV00015B/1584